W9-CHE-488

EXPLORING CAREERS

Computer Animator

Peggy J. Parks

KIDHAVEN PRESS
An imprint of Thomson Gale, a part of The Thomson Corporation

Detroit • New York • San Francisco • San Diego
New Haven, Conn.• Waterville, Maine • London • Munich

For more information, contact
KidHaven Press
27500 Drake Rd.
Farmington Hills, MI 48331-3535
Or you can visit our Internet site at http://www.gale.com

LIBRARY OF CONGRESS CATALOGING-IN-PUBLICATION DATA

Parks, Peggy J., 1951–
Computer animator / by Peggy J. Parks.
p. cm. — (Exploring careers)
Includes bibliographical references and index.
ISBN 0-7377-2065-4 (hard cover : alk. paper) 1. Computer animation—Vocational guidance—Juvenile literature. I. Title. II. Exploring careers (KidHaven Press)
TR897.7.P383 2005
006.6'96'023—dc22

2005016056

Printed in the United States of America

CONTENTS

CHAPTER 1

Types of Computer Animators

Computer animation is a magical kind of technology. It brings characters and scenery to life, making them look so real that viewers might forget they are looking at something that is make-believe. Computer animation can make bugs dance, fish sing, and cartoon people run, hop, jump, skip, and spin around in circles.

Computer animation has many practical uses, too. It can help people study and learn about the human body. It can also be used for designing cars and solving crimes. The potential of using computers for animation is amazing—and computer animators are the people who make it happen.

Fun and Games

Computer animators work in many different kinds of places. Those who create animated movies such as *The Incredibles* or *Robots* are employed by Pixar, Dreamworks, Blue Sky, or other well-known animation houses. When these studios create a movie, they often assign many computer animators to work on it. For example, as many as 50 Pixar animators were involved in making the movie *Finding Nemo*. To make the movie's characters seem believable, the animators spent time observing real fish. They went on diving trips in California and Hawaii.

Pictured here are two of the believable fish characters computer animators created for the animated film *Shark Tale*.

They studied the movements of tropical fish and learned about their mysterious world under the sea. They also spent time studying the fish in Pixar's own 25-gallon (95-liter) aquarium.

In addition to large studios, there are also many small companies that employ computer animators. Jellyvision in Chicago, Illinois, for instance, specializes in videogames. Jellyvision is known for such games as "You Don't Know Jack" and "Who Wants to Be a Millionaire?" Another small animation studio is Buzzco Associates in New York. Buzzco creates animated commercials, short films, and educational materials. One of the studio's commercials was for the Nick Jr. show *Maggie and the Ferocious Beast.*

A large number of computer animators are self-employed and are known as **freelancers**. They are hired for individual job assignments. Brian Larson is a freelance computer animator from Portland, Oregon. Larson has helped create animated television shows for the Disney Channel and the Cartoon Network. He also works on animated commercials for television. One of his spots was for Kellogg's Frosted Flakes cereal. It featured Tony the Tiger competing in a bicycle race with real kids.

Saving Lives

Entertainment is a very popular field with computer animators. But they work in many other areas as well. For instance, some computer animators

Many computer animators are self-employed and work as freelancers on individual job assignments.

specialize in creating materials that teach people about disease. Because cameras cannot physically record how disease affects the human body, animation is an excellent way to simulate it.

A company called Biochemical Animations created a short film about how mosquitoes carry the malaria disease. It used animation to show a mosquito biting a person and then illustrated how the insect's saliva traveled through the human body to attack blood cells. Computer animators also created a film that demonstrated a deadly infection known as anthrax. Some of Biochemical's animated films are used on television networks such as the Discovery Channel.

LifeHouse Productions in Connecticut also creates animated educational films. One LifeHouse production shows the intricate process of how blood clots. It also uses animation to explain what happens when people suffer from hemophilia, a disease that can lead to uncontrolled bleeding.

Eyes in Space

Another area of specialty for computer animators is simulating what occurs during space missions. Dan Maas, who owns a company called Maas Digital, produces animated videos for the National Aeronautics and Space Administration (NASA). Maas has been experimenting with animation since he was about ten years old. One of his videos showed the Mars Exploration Rover landing in 2004. He used a variety of blueprints, sketches, and graphics to create computer-generated images. Then he made them come alive through animation. It was a

A computer animator puts the finishing touches on an image of Saturn and the Voyager space probe for a NASA video.

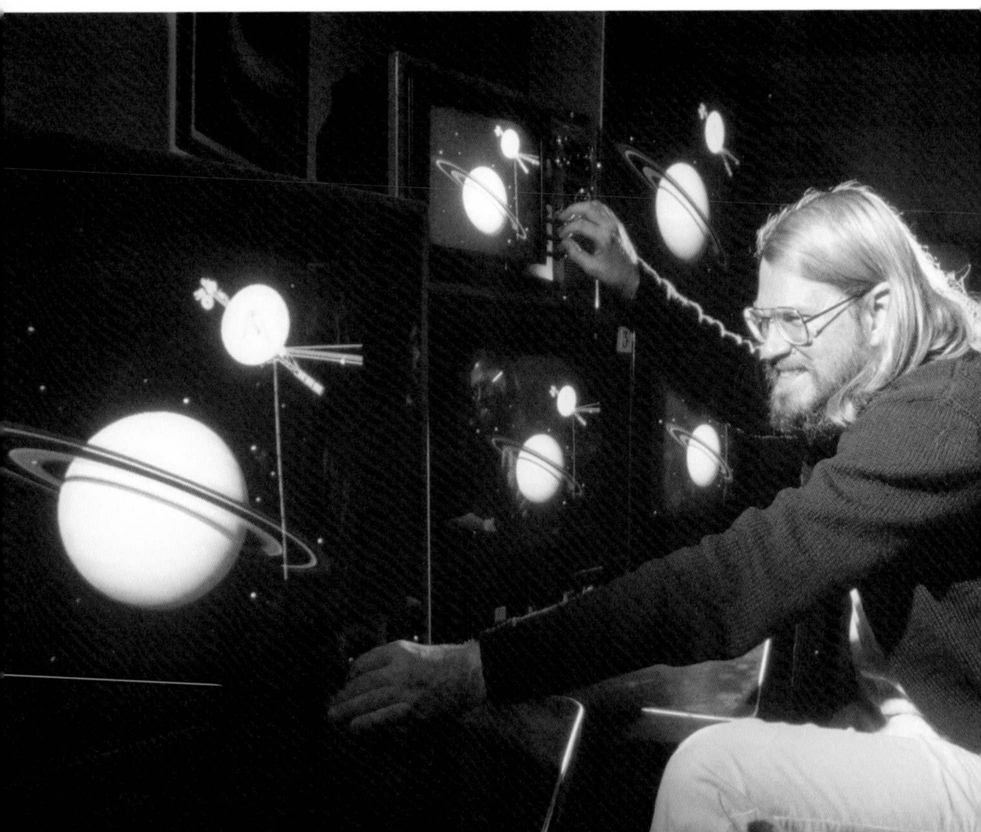

challenging project. "This really isn't that different from the processes Hollywood uses to make CGI [computer graphics imagery] for movies," he says. "The difference is that I'm illustrating actual space missions, not science fiction stories."[1]

Maas's video showed the spacecraft blasting off and then zooming through the atmosphere. As it drew closer to Mars, an enormous parachute unfurled and a massive cluster of airbags inflated. Like a giant rubber ball, the spacecraft's lander dropped to the ground and bounced over and over and over again. When it finally came to a stop, the airbags deflated. Then the lander slowly opened like the petals of a flower. Although this is what happened during the space mission, no one actually saw the landing. But people who viewed Maas's video could easily feel like they had witnessed the exciting event for themselves.

Courtroom Drama

Some computer animators devote their talents and skills to help solve crime or aid in accident investigations. One Arlington, Texas, company that specializes in this type of animation work is called 21st Century Forensic Animations. Its animated presentations are used during court trials. André Stuart, the firm's owner and a **forensic** animator, explains how such products are used: "An animation is not a film of actual events. It's a tool to help the jury visualize what happened, nothing more."[2]

One of 21st Century's productions was a 72-second video that re-created a murder. A man in Pennsylvania had shot his wife and claimed it was in self-defense. Using police testimony as their guide, the animators showed the man walking into the room and shooting his wife three times. There was no evidence that she had tried to harm him first. Defense attorney Paul Walker explains his reaction when he watched the video: "I've seen a lot of photos of people lying bloody on the ground. But when I saw the animation, it was eerie."[3] The animated video helped convince the jury of the man's crime. He was found guilty and sentenced to life in prison.

More Specialties

In addition to entertainment, medicine, and crime solving, computer animators work in many other fields. For example, architectural firms use them to create animations of buildings. Potential customers can "stroll through" rooms on a computer screen before a structure is ever built. Computer animators work for greeting card companies such as Hallmark. They create animated "e-cards" with characters that talk, sing, dance, and play instruments. Car makers use animators to create presentations that show the various safety features of cars and trucks. Computer animators also create videos for sports trainers to use when helping athletes perfect their techniques and improve their performance. And meteorologists

A scientific animator works on a short video that shows what happens to the molecules of a particular metal when it is heated.

use animation technology to study severe storms and weather patterns.

Whether they create blockbuster movies, videos of spacecraft landings, or animated re-creations that help solve crimes, computer animators are people who love their jobs. They use their skills, talents, and creativity to create realistic productions of all kinds. They work hard, and their days are often long, but most of them agree they could not imagine doing anything else. Glenn McQueen, who works for Pixar, explains how he feels about what he does for a living: "I do have the best job in the world, no question. Everybody should be jealous. This is so what you want to do."[4]

CHAPTER 2

What It Takes to Be a Computer Animator

Of all the people who work as computer animators, very few have followed the exact same career path. Some have experimented with computers for years and have taught themselves much of what they know. Others have studied in colleges that offer specialized programs. No matter how their careers began, people who work in this field share one thing in common: They have long been fascinated by the amazing possibilities of computer animation.

Animation and Art

Something else computer animators have in common is their interest in art. Even though animated productions are created on computers, being a technology whiz is not enough. Most computer animators say that drawing skills are essential. This is true whether they specialize in animated movies, educational presentations, space exploration videos, or any other type of production. By sketching their ideas on paper first, animators are able to visualize what their finished creation will look like.

Many computer animators started drawing at a very young age. This was the case with Jack Heiter, a well-known animator who has worked on hit television shows such as *Rugrats*. Heiter says that as a child, he spent hours copying pictures from comic strips and comic books. Because his family

A team of computer animators reviews a series of sketches and drawings of characters they plan to feature in an animated film.

was poor, he did not have money to buy special art paper. So, he drew on whatever he could find—paper bags, the backs of letters, the borders of schoolbooks, and even the white top of his mother's kitchen table. In high school Heiter studied art, and his teacher encouraged him to start creating original characters. He used his artistic talent to become a cartoonist for his school newspaper. Later, his art experience and training helped lead him into a successful computer animation career.

Young people interested in a career in computer animation should learn how to use computer animation software.

Frank Gladstone, who has worked for major studios such as Disney, Warner Brothers, and DreamWorks, agrees that drawing talent is a must for computer animators. He says that some talent is natural, but it takes constant practice to develop it. Gladstone advises young people to visit zoos and sketch the animals or to draw pictures of their friends and family. Through regular drawing, aspiring animators learn to create realistic characters and scenery as well as action and movement—all of which are at the heart of computer animation. Gladstone explains why drawing skills are so important: "Computer animators just have a very fancy electronic pencil. If they can draw traditionally, they're that much ahead of the game."[5] He recommends that young people who want to become animators take all the art classes that are offered in high school. That includes not only drawing but also other types of art such as painting and sculpting. Becoming accomplished artists will help them be better animators.

Learning the Trade

In addition to art training, young people can benefit from learning how to use computer animation software. There are Web sites that can help with this. One example is Amazing Kids! Animation Station!, which is designed especially for kids. The site includes step-by-step tutorials for working with the popular animation program called Flash.

Another feature of the site is a contest for students from ages six to seventeen. Participants can create and submit their own animated productions. Past winners have received free software as well as valuable tips from Gladstone and other well-known animation professionals.

After high school, Gladstone urges aspiring animators to earn a college degree. Even though studios do not necessarily require animators to have a degree, the animation field has become extremely popular. That means competition for the best jobs is fierce. This competitiveness is emphasized in the Web site Animation Arena, which explains, "You are just like an actor auditioning for a part. Everyone wants the part, you have to want it more than anyone else, so much so that they couldn't cast anyone else but you for the role."[6]

People interested in studying computer animation often enroll in colleges with specialized programs. One such school is the Ringling School of Art and Design in Sarasota, Florida. Students spend their first year studying art and design. Then they move into intensive animation studies, including character development, lighting, motion, and sound. Along the way they learn how to create **storyboards**, which serve as a master plan or blueprint for an animated film or other production. They also sharpen their technical skills by working with animation software. Toward the end of the program, students put

A graphic artist creates a storyboard that outlines the sequence of events in his animated film.

their talents and training to work by creating their own short animated film.

One advantage for students who attend special computer animation programs is the professional contacts they make. Ringling, for example, often hosts recruiters from major studios such as Pixar, Industrial Light & Magic, DreamWorks, and Blue Sky, as well as representatives from Hallmark Cards, the Weather Channel, the Discovery Channel, Nickelodeon, and others. College seniors have a chance to talk with these industry professionals and show them their art portfolios. They can also gain information about internships and apprenticeships that might be available. These provide students with valuable on-the-job training in the computer animation field.

Showing Off

In addition to meeting computer animation professionals, there is another important benefit of attending specialty colleges: Students learn how to create a **demo reel**. This is a videotape or DVD that shows a few minutes of the person's best work. Often, an aspiring animator's reel is the first (and sometimes only) chance to get noticed by a possible employer. If it does not show talent and originality, it will simply be thrown away. Veteran animator Peter Konig reviews demo reels on a regular basis. He says that most of them are very poorly done: "One out of a hundred is decent, no joke. . . . All I care about is the quality of the work. . . . I don't even look at the resume or credentials until I've seen the demo tape or DVD. If it isn't any good, I don't really care where they went to school."[7]

Aspiring computer animators may also gain exposure for their work by entering contests. Morgan Kelly, who graduated from the California Institute of the Arts, created his own short animated film called "The Terrible Tragedy of Virgil and Maurice."

As part of their training, young computer animation students learn the basics of human anatomy.

The film won awards—but more importantly, it caught the attention of DreamWorks. The studio was so impressed that Kelly was accepted in DreamWorks's animation training program. For ten weeks Kelly worked with experienced computer animators. He was trained to use the studio's animation software, and he also learned about the production process involved in creating a major film. After his training was finished, Kelly was hired by DreamWorks to work on the film *Shrek 2*.

Computer animators are people with many talents and skills. They believe art is extremely important, and most have been drawing since they were children. They encourage young people who dream of being animators to practice drawing, become familiar with animation software, and look into colleges with specialized programs. In spite of tough competition, those who want animation careers badly enough—and are willing to work hard to achieve their dream—have a chance of making it. Konig offers these words of encouragement: "Do it because you love it, work hard to become fantastic at it. If you stand out, if you're tough and resourceful and persistent, you'll have a great chance to do it for a living. . . . Get a strong background in the basics, and move on from there. . . . Do I sound like a dad or what? Stop reading this and get back to work!"[8]

CHAPTER 3

Computer Animators at Work

What computer animators do from day to day depends on their particular specialty. Some of them spend hours poring over police reports and crime scene evidence, while others study movie or television scripts and meet with film directors. Animators may work by themselves in home offices or work as part of a team in large animation studios. But even though they have different types of jobs, all computer animators have the same goal: combining art and technology to turn ideas into believable finished products.

A computer animator moves frame by frame through his film, which features animated rams playing football.

Making a Movie

Computer animators who work on feature films create every second of the action that viewers see on a movie screen—and accomplishing that is a massive job. They use sophisticated animation software to arrange (or choreograph) the movements of the film's characters. This includes not only action-type movements such as walking, running, hopping, or dancing, but also all facial gestures. Any time characters blink, smile, frown, yawn, or stick their tongues out, computer animators made those gestures happen. In addition, animators control the movement of scenery in a film.

If there is supposed to be a hurricane, for instance, it is the animators who make trees bend over and debris fly around in the wind. Because of their ability to control movement, animators are often called digital puppeteers. Blue Sky Studios explains this: "Animating a character in the computer is like moving around a puppet; for every movement or action the animator will pose the character using a variety of controls that move the head, hips, arms, feet and legs, and countless other details to build a performance."[9]

Computer animators start by reading the movie script one or more times. This helps them get to know the characters and understand what they are supposed to do. They also study the storyboards and listen to the dialogue, which has been recorded in a studio with professional actors. The way the actors speak their lines often influences how the animators will make their characters act on the screen.

After the images have been scanned into the computer, the animators create a series of **frames** that show movement in various steps. Each frame shows just one small and subtle change. One example is a scene in *Robots* that showed the character Big Weld with his arm around Rodney. In the first frame, animators put Big Weld's arm at his side. In the next frame, his arm starts to rise. By the final frame, his arm stretches around Rodney. Computer animation technology causes these pictures to flash one after the other very rapidly on the screen—24 times per second. The result is an illusion of movement that looks continuous and perfectly smooth to the viewer.

Animating Space Missions

The process that Dan Mass follows when he creates videos is similar to that of animators who work on movies. But he is not handed a script or storyboards—he creates them on his own. Long before he begins working on a video, Maas spends many hours gathering information. He meets with NASA engineers and scientists. He asks them questions about the structure of a spacecraft, the route it will take into space, and the celestial bodies it will pass during its journey. He also studies plans, photographs, diagrams, and blueprints. By the time his research is finished, Maas thoroughly understands every single detail of an upcoming space mission.

His first step in creating a video is to imagine what the final product will look like. Then he begins putting his ideas on paper by drawing the storyboard. He draws separate panels to represent the different scenes of a mission. If he is happy with the storyboards, he creates an **animatic** on his computer. An animatic is a very rough, simple video animation. It does not show finished objects such as spacecraft, rockets, or planets. Instead, Maas first represents these objects with simple shapes like spheres and boxes. He takes the animatic to NASA to get his client's comments and

Using computer animation, a NASA scientist describes in detail how the Mars Rover landed safely on Mars in 2004.

suggestions. Then he returns to his office and starts the finish work.

Maas uses several types of computer programs to create his animated videos. For instance, computer-aided design software allows him to build three-dimensional objects such as the Mars Exploration Rover. He adds details to the spacecraft with special painting software. He uses a different type of software for **rendering**, which is the finished art that makes all images look crisp, real, and perfect. Maas says rendering is the most time-consuming task of all. He spends as much as an hour rendering each frame—and because 24 frames are needed for each second of a video, the rendering process alone can take weeks.

Animating a Crime

When forensic animators create videos, their process is similar to the one used by Maas. But instead of reviewing scientific data, they research the evidence of a case. When there has been an accident or a crime, for instance, forensic animators study the investigation data. They read police and coroner reports, statements from witnesses, and vehicle inspections. They also review photographs and medical reports. Once they have thoroughly reviewed the evidence, they prepare storyboards. Then they begin creating the presentation on the computer.

Forensic animators first create the scene of the crime or other environment where the action took place. Using drawing software, they build models of whatever objects are needed, such as humans or vehicles. Then they add color, texture, and other details to make the objects look as much like their real-life counterparts as possible. For example, when André Stuart created his video showing the Pennsylvania murder, he studied photographs of the victim. He wanted to make the computer model look like the

A computer animator works with special software that allows him to design three-dimensional models of spacecraft.

A forensic animator creates a computer model of a female victim in a criminal case.

woman did in real life, so he gave her sandy-blond hair and wire-rimmed glasses and dressed her in the animal-print pajamas she wore that day.

The final steps in creating forensic animation are much the same as the steps taken in any animated film or video. Animators add details, render the characters and scenery, choreograph the action, and then fine-tune the presentation. But unlike productions that are designed for entertainment, the focus of forensic animation is not on creativity—it is on accuracy. If an animated production is not completely accurate, it might not be usable as evidence in court. That could result in an important case being dismissed or a guilty criminal getting away with a crime.

Different Specialties, Different Tasks

Just as no two animated productions are exactly the same, no two computer animators do exactly the same job. Their tasks vary based on where they work and what types of productions they create. They may read movie scripts, compile scientific research data, or study the evidence of an accident or crime. Some of them choreograph the actions of movie monsters, while others show step-by-step details of a real-life crime. They may work in animation studios, police departments, or home offices. Wherever they work and whatever their jobs involve, computer animators strive to create animated productions that are believable to viewers.

CHAPTER 4

Meet a Computer Animator

When Dylan Brown is in his office, he is never alone. All around him are strange, colorful fish with names like Dory, Marlin, and Bruce. These fish are not real, of course, because they can talk, laugh, and crack jokes. They only exist on computer monitors or movie screens—but they are so realistic that they almost seem to be alive. That is because of the magic of computer animation, which is what Brown does for a living. He is a supervising animator with Pixar Animation Studios.

In 1985 a computer animator works on an ad for MTV that features robotic dinosaurs.

The Aspiring Animator

Brown first became interested in computer animation when he saw the movie *Jurassic Park* in 1993. He had a computer at home, but he could not afford animation software because it costs thousands of dollars. So he called companies that make the software and talked them into sending him demo tapes. When they arrived, he spent hours studying and experimenting with them. "From that point on I was hooked,"[10] he says. He was eager to learn more about computer animation, and he found out that San Francisco State University had a program that specializes in it.

But he also learned that getting in would not be easy. The school required a portfolio of animation work, and he did not have one. "It was weird," he says. "The reason I wanted to go there was to learn about animation—but because I didn't already know how to animate, they weren't going to let me in to learn about it!" Finally, he convinced the school to accept him into the program and he began taking classes.

Toys, Bugs, and Monsters

In 1995 Brown became aware that Pixar was developing a videogame based on the movie *Toy Story*. The studio needed extra people, and he was hired to do technical work on the CD-ROM. On nights when he did not have class, he went into the studio and worked with the animation software. Eventually, he decided to quit school so he could devote all his attention to Pixar. "I went to SF [San Francisco] State for a year and a half and I learned a lot," he says. "But the hands-on experience I was gaining at Pixar was so much more valuable to me. I don't remember a time in my life when I soaked up information like that, but once I discovered animation, my brain became a sponge. I learned so much, so fast, and just could not seem to get enough of it."

In 1996 Brown completed a training program at Pixar and then worked on the animation team for *A Bug's Life*. His next two movies were *Toy Story 2* and *Monsters, Inc.* "Working on those three movies was such an incredible experience," he says. "I learned the importance of making the characters come to life—to make them seem real to people watching the movie. With every new challenge, I grew to love animation even more."

The Challenges of *Finding Nemo*

By the time Pixar was ready to do a film about a curious little clownfish named Nemo, Brown had gained enough experience to be supervising animator. "Leading the animation team for *Finding Nemo* was challenging as well as exciting, and without a doubt the best learning experience of all.

Pictured here is a model of Nemo, the animated clownfish that Dylan Brown and his Pixar team created for the film *Finding Nemo*.

Cofounder of Apple Computer and Pixar Animation, Steve Jobs (far left) meets with his animation team to discuss the progress of their projects.

I did some of the animating myself and was also responsible for the overall work of the team."

Finding Nemo posed greater challenges for the animators than any other film they had done, and Brown explains why:

> Unlike the characters in previous Pixar films, our friends Dory, Marlin, Bruce, and the others, didn't have traditional bodies because they were fish. We had an entire cast of characters with no arms or legs! It was easier with a character like Woody in the movie *Toy Story*. When we wanted to show that Woody was sad, we simply made

> his shoulders slump. In *Finding Nemo*, we needed to show Marlin's great sadness because his son had been taken away—but fish do not have shoulders to slump! So we had to make up for that by overexaggerating facial expressions and by changing how the fish moved while they were swimming.

Brown says that creating natural-looking characters is one of the greatest challenges for any animator. "We're constantly striving to make characters and scenery look natural and organic rather than robotic and mechanical. That is an ongoing process that requires fixing, adjusting, and polishing."

The Life of an Animator

Brown says that an animator's day typically starts with meetings that are called animation dailies. This is where the team gets together to review progress that has been made on a film. The group sits in a screening room that is about half the size of a normal movie theater. "When we're working on a movie," he says, "we're all working on different scenes, and sometimes several of us are working on the same scene. The dailies help us see and critique each other's work on a big screen, where gestures and facial expressions are easier to see than on a small desktop computer. When you're talking about a major animated movie, even the smallest details are important."

After the daily is over the animators go back to their offices, where they spend the rest of the day creating a movie's animated sequences. This involves matching the characters' actions with their voices, which have been prerecorded by professional actors. According to Brown, this is very time-consuming work. From start to finish, creating *Finding Nemo* took about three years, and that meant long hours and hard work for the animation team. Brown says that Pixar helps people cope with work-related stress by encouraging a playful atmosphere:

> They [Pixar executives] know how easy it is to get burned out, so they make sure the work environment is fun and relaxed. Take, for example, one day when we were in the middle of *Finding Nemo*. All of a sudden everyone just started climbing up on the wall partitions (which are 12 feet [4m] high), and leaping off them to land face first on the beanbag couches below. We were acting like a bunch of kids, but I believe far too many people forget how to be kids once they grow up. One thing is for sure—around here no one has forgotten that!

A computer animator with Pixar takes a break by juggling, while his coworker relaxes with Woody, a character from *Toy Story*.

Advice for Young People

When asked whether he would recommend a career in computer animation, Brown says there is no better job on Earth—but he also stresses that it is extremely hard work:

> People see cool animation on the big screen and they think it looks so easy. Well, the reason it looks easy is because we put so much time and effort into making it look that way. For the right person—someone who has the right combination of creativity, motivation, and willingness to work very hard—computer animation is a fabulous career. It is definitely tough to break into the field because it's so competitive, but I can't possibly imagine a more fulfilling job.

Brown says his greatest moment as an animator was when *Finding Nemo* was finally done and he went to see it at the theater:

> I was there as just another member of the audience and no one knew who I was. I watched people's reactions, and when I saw how much they loved the movie, how much they got into it, I wanted to stand up and shout, "Hey everyone, I did that!" Of all the moments in an artist's career, nothing can compare with seeing other people enjoy and appreciate your work. It is, by far, the ultimate high.

NOTES

Chapter 1: Types of Computer Animators

1. Dan Maas, interview with author, August 17, 2005.
2. André Stuart, "Seeing Is Believing: Forensic Animation Sheds Light on the Truth," *Professional Surveyor*, April 2001. www.call21st.com/surveyor1.htm.
3. Quoted in Jacob Ward, "Crime Seen," *Wired*, May 2002. www.call21st.com/wired1.htm.
4. Quoted in Kenneth Plume, "Interview with Pixar Animator Glenn McQueen," *FilmForce*, February 10, 2000. http://filmforce.ign.com/articles/035/035856p1.htm.

Chapter 2: What It Takes to Be a Computer Animator

5. Quoted in Shanna Smith, "So You Wanna Be an Animator?" Animation Arena. www.animationarena.com/become-an-animator.html.

6. Animation Arena, "Choosing an Animation School." www.animationarena.com/choosing-an-animation-school.html.
7. Quoted in Animation Arena, "3D Modeler: Peter Konig." www.animationarena.com/3d-modeler.html.
8. Quoted in Animation Arena, "3D Modeler."

Chapter 3: Computer Animators at Work

9. Blue Sky Studios, "Our Process: Animation." www.blueskystudios.com/content/process-animation.php.

Chapter 4: Meet a Computer Animator

10. All quotes in Chapter 4: Dylan Brown, interview with author, December 10, 2003.

GLOSSARY

animatic: A rough, simple video animation.

demo reel: A videotape or DVD that presents a computer animator's best work.

forensic: Applying science to the law, especially in connection with solving crimes.

frames: Still images in an animated production. When frames flash rapidly on the screen, it gives the illusion of movement.

freelancers: Professionals who are self-employed.

rendering: The process of creating finished art for a movie, video, or other animated production.

storyboards: Master plans that use a comic book style to show the characters and action steps in a movie or other production.

FOR FURTHER EXPLORATION

Books

Stephen Cole, *The Incredibles: The Essential Guide*. New York: DK, 2004. Written for young people, this book gives readers an inside glimpse at the making of the blockbuster animated film *The Incredibles*.

———, *Shrek: The Essential Guide*. New York: DK, 2004. Another behind-the-scenes book for young readers, this one discusses the hit movie *Shrek*.

Internet Sources

Sean Russell, "How TV Animation Works," *Stuffo: How Stuff Works*. http://stuffo.howstuffworks.com/tv-animation.htm.

Jeff Tyson, "How Industrial Light & Magic Works," *Stuffo: How Stuff Works*. http://stuffo.howstuffworks.com/perfect-storm.htm.

Periodicals

Jeanna Bryner, "Movie Magic: Go Behind the Scenes of *Robots* to Discover the Secrets to Creating

Smash-Hit Animations," *Science World*, March 28, 2005.

Ross Workman, "Behind the Scenes of the Movie 'Robots,'" *Time for Kids*, March 7, 2005.

Web Sites

Amazing Kids! Animation Station!
(www.amazing-kids.org/anistation1.htm). This site is excellent for young people who are interested in learning about computer animation. It includes tips and suggestions, resources, and information about contests that aspiring animators can enter. It also includes a showcase of animation work by past contest winners.

Animation Arena
(www.animationarena.com). This Web site contains a vast collection of valuable information about the animation field, including articles, interviews, and advice about education and training.

Blue Sky Studios
(www.blueskystudios.com). This is a good resource for the aspiring animator. There is information about Blue Sky's process, including descriptions of individual team members and what tools they use.

Pixar Animation Studios
(www.pixar.com). Pixar's Web site is another good

resource for young people interested in exploring the field of animation. In addition to interviews with Pixar animation professionals, the site also includes a "How We Make a Movie" feature that covers the various steps in the animation process.

INDEX

PICTURE CREDITS

Cover: Gale Zucker/Blackbirch Press Archives

© Bob Rowan; Progressive Image/CORBIS, 17
© Chuck Savage/CORBIS, 19
© Dan Lamont/CORBIS, 28
© Douglas Kirkland/CORBIS, 34
© Dreamworks Animation/Bureau of L.A. Collections/CORBIS, 5
© Fred Greaves/Reuters/CORBIS, 25
Gale Zucker/Blackbirch Press Archives, 7, 13 (both), 22, 27
© Jim Sugar/CORBIS
© Karl Larsen/ZUMA/CORBIS, 33
© Roger Ressmeyer/CORBIS, 8, 11, 31
© Royalty-Free/CORBIS, 14

ABOUT THE AUTHOR

Peggy J. Parks holds a bachelor of science degree from Aquinas College in Grand Rapids, Michigan, where she graduated magna cum laude. She has written more than 40 titles for Thomson Gale's KidHaven Press, Blackbirch Press, and Lucent Books imprints. Parks lives in Muskegon, Michigan, a town she says inspires her writing because of its location on the shores of Lake Michigan.